Prue's Tea Party

By Carmel Reilly

Prue will have a tea party.

All her dolls and her teddy
will be at the party.

Her friend Kirk will come, too.

Prue will make a new sort of tea.

The tea is named True Blue.

It's in a cute blue box.

Kirk is due to come at ten.

Prue looks at the clock.

She has lots of time
to set up.

She puts a blue cloth
on her desk.

She sets out her best cups.

They have two blue birds
on them.

At last, Kirk is here.

Prue tips the tea pot.

She serves True Blue tea
for Kirk and for her teddy.

Kirk takes a sip of tea.

He loves True Blue!

"It's so good, Prue!"
he says.
"The dolls must try it, too!"

Kirk gets up to tip some tea
for the dolls, but he is too quick.

He drops the pot on the cup,
and the cup breaks!

Kirk goes still like a statue.

Prue gets a shock,
but she is not sad.

"I'm so sorry!" Kirk says.
"I will get you a new cup!"

"No! It's fine, Kirk!" says Prue.

"But I feel bad," says Kirk.

"Please don't argue, Kirk!" says Prue.

Prue gets a new cup
for her dolls.

They all think True Blue
is great tea!

CHECKING FOR MEANING

1. Who was at Prue's tea party? *(Literal)*

2. What was the name of the tea they drank at the tea party? *(Literal)*

3. Why did Kirk go still like a statue when he broke the cup? *(Inferential)*

EXTENDING VOCABULARY

cute	What does *cute* mean? Do you own anything that could be described as cute? What makes it cute?
due	What does it mean when we say something is *due*? Can you think of a sentence that uses this word? E.g. *My homework is due on Friday.*
argue	What does it mean to *argue*? Have you ever argued with a friend? What did you argue about? Why?

MOVING BEYOND THE TEXT

1. Does your family invite friends to have a cup of tea or coffee at your house? Why?

2. What other reasons do you visit other people's homes or have people visit you?

3. What other types of parties do we have? E.g. pizza party, birthday party, pool party.

4. Have you ever broken something valuable that belonged to a friend? What happened? How did you feel?

SPEED SOUNDS

oo	ue	ew	ui	u_e
ou	u	oe	o	

PRACTICE WORDS

Prue

too

new

True

Blue

cute

due

to

statue

argue

true

you